Th
ME

IN 7 EASY STEPS

7 Easy Lessons & Exercises   for Beginners!

Understanding the Teachings of Eckhart Tolle, Krishnamurti,
Maharishi Mahesh Yogi and more!

A. J. PARR

THE SECRET OF NOW SERIES
GRAPEVINE BOOKS
2017

A. J. P A R R

DISCLAIMER

AUTHOR:

A. J. Parr. See Amazon Author Page

COVER PHOTO:

Wikimedia Commons

PUBLISHED BY:

Grapevine Books (Ediciones De La Parra)

ISBN-13: 978-1542598316

ISBN-10: 1542598311

C O N T E N T

FOREWORD

"Meditation can wipe away the day's stress, bringing with it inner peace... Meditation can give you a sense of calm, peace and balance that benefits both your emotional well-being and your overall health. And these benefits don't end when your meditation session ends. Meditation can help carry you more calmly through your day and may improve certain medical conditions (from anxiety disorders, asthma and depression, to cancer, heart disease and high blood pressure)"

Mayo Clinic Report*"*

THESE PAGES CONTAIN the basic lessons and exercises you need to learn how to meditate today and begin to experience a more joyful and peaceful life. They are the ′product of three decades of my own meditation practice and Comparative Religion research, considering the ancient holistic principle that *"in essence there is and always has been only one spiritual teaching, although it comes in many forms"*, as expressed by the German-Canadian spiritual teacher Eckhart Tolle, author of the best-seller *"The Power of Now"*, and as evidenced by the teachings of the 14th Dalai Lama, Krishnamurti, Ramana Maharshi, Swami Vivekananda, Swami Sivananda, and Maharishi Mahesh Yogi, among other meditation masters briefly cited in this training book.

If you're wondering if you need to change your present beliefs or religion to practice meditation, the answer is: No way! This teaching is open to people of all creeds interested in learning a quick way of experiencing inner peace and discovering the joy of living.

Of course, we all eventually have ups and downs in life and that′s not going to change. But if you start meditating and learn how to calm your mind you will start seeing things with a clear mind and gradually develop discernment and peace of mind, which is a clear advantage whenever times go wrong.

WHAT THIS BOOK CAN SHOW YOU:

Why the chattering mind is often compared with a wild animal.

How our mind creates our own suffering, grief, anger, worries and desolation.

What "mantra meditation" and how it is used to easily train the mind.

How to practice the basic steps of mantra meditation.

What to face our thoughts during meditation.

How to recognize the illusory nature of our "false self" during meditation.

How to meet our "true Self" and experience inner stillness during meditation.

How to face stressful situations, avoid excessive worries and keep a clear mind whenever times go wrong.

How to experience inner stillness and peace of mind.

And more!

BENEFITS OF MEDITATION PRACTICE

Hundreds of research studies evidence the physical and psychological benefits of meditation practice, published in scientific journals and conducted at prestigious universities and research centers like the Harvard Medical School, Yale Medical School, UCLA Medical School, Stanford Medical School, and Medical College of Georgia.

As universal practice, it constitutes the spinal cord of the world's oldest Religions, from Hinduism and Buddhism, to Chinese Taoism and primitive Christianity, among the most known.

It was first popularized in America and Europe during the late 1800s and early 1900s, and experienced an unprecedented boost in the 1960s, when the Beatles and other celebrities turned to the Indian physicist and spiritual leader Maharishi Mahesh Yogi, founder of the Transcendental Meditation movement, known as TM.

According to ancient teachings, the transcendental object of meditation is to help us *"wake up"* from the hypnotic dream of illusion or *"Maya"*, as the ancient Hindu and Buddhist sages called it.

Living under the influence of this illusion has been traditionally compared with the act of *"living in a dream"*. And the process of freeing ourselves from its grip with the act of *"waking up"* or *"awakening."*

This is why the name Buddha literally means the *"Awakened One"*.

Eckhart Tolle calls this process *"the awakening of consciousness from the dream of matter, form, and separation"*.

He also claims that, unless we wake up, we are doomed to continue living under the veil of illusion.

Dalai Lama also compares our illusory reality, which only exists in our own heads, with a dream and also with the trick of a magician, as he states in his book *"Transcendent Wisdom"*:

> *"While dreaming, all kinds of things may come to mind, but these are nothing more than appearances. Likewise, a magician may create a variety of illusory appearances, but they do not exist objectively... "*

As Dalai Lama explains, one of the main principles of Buddhist wisdom is that your personal problems and suffering are always *"self-inflicted"*, mere creations of your own mind...

Meditation is not hard to learn. However, its effectiveness will always depend on you, that is, on your own practice and dedication.

Just like swimming, riding a bicycle or playing a musical instrument, learning to meditate depends on experience and not on strict theory. Only through practice and self-knowledge - and not through someone else´s words or experience - we can experience mental calmness and inner peace.

LESSON I

THE WANDERING MONKEY-MIND

"By night and by day, just like a monkey swinging from branch to branch reaches a forest on the side of a mountain, that which is called 'thought', 'mind' and 'cognition' arises and ceases, one after another..."

Gautama Buddha

A. J. P A R R

THE BASIC GOAL OF MEDITATION, according to the ancient teachings of Hinduism, is to produce or gestate the inner transformation that can allow us to free ourselves from the profound illusion that separates us from experiencing our true inner Being or higher Self.

To accomplish this, the first step consists in understanding what this illusion is and how it is continuously generated by our own thoughts, through an endless flow of *"inner chatter"* or *"internal dialogue"* that, as these pages reveal, literally keeps us trapped in a dream of falseness and delusion. Lost in our own thoughts, we perpetually fill our minds with thoughts of unhappiness, dissatisfaction and suffering, ignoring that the only true joy and satisfaction lies hidden within us.

THE MONKEY MIND

Buddha compared the thinking mind with a wild monkey that cannot stay still and is always jumping from branch to branch, that is, always jumping from one thought to another. This is why, according to an ancient Buddhist saying, *"you cannot understand enlightenment with the monkey mind."*

The Nineteenth Century wandering Hindu monk known as Swami Vivekananda, who in 1893 received a standing ovation from 7,000 people at the World's Parliament of Religions, held in Chicago, also compared the human mind with a wild monkey and claimed that true liberation can only result from freeing ourselves from its untamed influence.

To *"tame"* it, Vivekananda recommended starting out by *"watching the mind"* or *"observing the mind"*, a practice he described as follows:

> *"The first lesson is to sit for some time and let the mind run on. The mind is bubbling up all the time. It is like that monkey jumping about. Let the monkey jump as much as he can; you simply wait and watch.*

> *"Knowledge is power, says the proverb, and that is true.*

> *"Until you know what the mind is doing you cannot control it. Give it the rein; many hideous thoughts may come into it; you will be astonished that it was possible for you to think such thoughts.*

> *"But you will find that each day the mind's vagaries are becoming less and less violent, that each day it is becoming calmer..."*

Vivekananda sustained that without proper training, you can never get to free yourself from the undesired influence of your monkey mind. And teaching you how to begin to accomplish this is what these pages are all about!

Taming the monkey mind was one of the basic objectives pursued by the Buddha, who proclaimed that *"we are what we think"* and that only by recognizing the illusory nature of our thoughts and beliefs through periodical inner observation and meditation, we can escape from the grasps of the world of Illusion and experience our true Self in the Now.

According to the Buddhist scriptures known as the *Assutavā Sutta*, Buddha once said:

> *"By night and by day that which is called 'thought', 'mind' and 'cognition' arises and ceases, one after another. By night and by day, just like a monkey swinging from branch to branch reaches a forest on the side of a mountain, that which is called 'thought', 'mind' and 'cognition' arises and ceases, one after another..."*

In another occasion, according to the *Adanta Sutra*, the Buddha highlighted the importance of avoiding "the perils of the untamed mind":

> *"Monks, I know not of any other single thing so conducive to great loss as the untamed mind. The untamed mind indeed conduces to great loss. Monks, I know not of any other single thing so conducive to great profit as the tamed mind. The tamed mind indeed conduces to great profit".*

It is believed that the one-word Chinese term *"mind-monkey"* (*"xinyuan"*) was first coined by Zen Buddhist monks in the early 6th century. Since then, it officially serves to describe the *"unsettled and incontrollable mind that is constantly jumping, constantly agitated, constantly distracted and repeatedly racing without stop"*.

On his behalf, the celebrated Hindu guru Swami Sivananda Saraswati (1887-1963), founder of the Divine Life Society and the Yoga-Vedanta Forest Academy, once explained:

> *"The mind in the vast majority of persons has been allowed to run wild and follow its own sweet will and desire.*

*"It is ever changing and wandering.
It jumps from one object to another.*

*"It is fickle. It wants variety.
Monotony brings disgust.*

*"It is like a spoiled child who is
given too much indulgence by its
parents or a badly trained animal."*

THE CHATTERING MIND

The philosopher and spiritual teacher from India Jiddu Krishnamurti (1895-1986) referred to the monkey mind as the *"chattering mind"*, stating that this chatter is a constant process, an endless operation, and that *"every moment it is murmuring"*.

In his best-selling 1954 book *"The First and Last Freedom"* he openly discussed what makes our minds chatter, where does the mind get the energy and what is the purpose of that chattering. Is it just like water flowing, like water running out of the tap? Krishnamurti concluded that the mind apparently needs to be occupied with something. And if it is not occupied, it feels vacant, it feels empty and therefore it resorts to chattering:

*"As I watch the brain, I see that the
chattering happens only in the brain, it
is a brain activity; a current flows up*

and down, but it is chaotic,
meaningless and purposeless. The
brain wears itself out by its own
activity. One can see that it is tiring to
the brain, but it does not stop... The
mind chatters all the time and the
energy devoted to that purpose fills a
major part of our life.

"The mind apparently needs to be
occupied with something... The mind is
occupied with something and if it is not
occupied, it feels vacant, it feels empty
and therefore it resorts to
chattering..."

What Krishnamurti called the *"chattering mind"* in the 1950s, Eckhart Tolle called the *"thinking mind"* in the nineties, explaining that it is the perpetual source of the endless *"mental chatter"* produced *"the voice in the head"*.

Eckhart Tolle explains that *"the voice in the head"* continuously comments, complains, guesses, judges, compares, approves and disapproves, all this seemingly on its own. But the truth is that it only follows an automatic mental process based on the repetition of what he calls *"unconscious mental-emotional reactive patterns"*.

DON'T LET YOUR MIND RUN WILD

It is believed that the one-word term *"mind-monkey"* was first coined in China by Zen Buddhist monks in the early 6th century (*"xinyuan"* in Chinese). In any case, according to Zen Buddhism, the term *"mind-monkey"* serves to describe the *"unsettled and incontrollable mind that is constantly jumping, constantly agitated, constantly distracted and repeatedly racing without stop"*.

On his behalf, the celebrated Hindu guru Swami Sivananda Saraswati (1887-1963), founder of the Divine Life Society and the Yoga-Vedanta Forest Academy, once explained:

> *"The mind in the vast majority of persons has been allowed to run wild and follow its own sweet will and desire.*
>
> *"It is ever changing and wandering. It jumps from one object to another.*
>
> *"It is fickle. It wants variety. Monotony brings disgust.*
>
> *"It is like a spoiled child who is given too much indulgence by its parents or a badly trained animal."*

To understand the basic workings of the monkey mind, Sivananda formulated the following four principles:

FIRST PRINCIPLE:

The minds of many of us are like menageries of wild animals, each pursuing the bent of its own nature and going its own way.

SECOND PRINCIPLE:

Restraint of the mind is a thing unknown to the vast majority of persons.

THIRD PRINCIPLE:

This wandering habit of the mind manifests itself in various ways.

FOURTH PRINCIPLE:

You will have to be alert always to check this wandering habit of the mind...

This state of *"alertness"*, as we shall see in these pages, basically consists in directing your attention to your wandering thoughts, that is, to the *"endless chatter"* generated by the *"monkey-mind"* and learning to differentiate it from *"the Silent Witness"* or your true Self.

EXERCISE ONE

MEETING THE MONKEY MIND

"One must know oneself as one is, not as one wishes to be which is merely an ideal and therefore fictitious, unreal. It is only that which is that can be transformed, not that which you wish to be. To know oneself as one is requires an extraordinary alertness of mind..."

Jiddu Krishnamurti

MOST PEOPLE BELIEVE they can actually control their minds. But most of them are wrong. Our minds are constantly creating thoughts beyond our direct control. And these thoughts are the product of involuntary processes based on *"automatic psychological responses or reactions"* produced unconsciously, that is, involuntarily and therefore beyond our conscious control.

Eckhart Tolle, as mentioned, says these reactions obey our *"unconscious mental-emotional reactive patterns"*.

In short words, this exercises evidences that just like certain chemicals react automatically whenever they reach contact, most of your continuous flow of thoughts is produced "automatically", without your conscious awareness or control.

Krishnamurti first announced that *"thinking is a reaction"* over half a century ago, in 1954, as he expressed in *"The First and Last Freedom"*:

> *"Surely thinking is a reaction. If I ask you a question, you respond to it - you respond according to your memory, to your prejudices, to your upbringing, to the climate, to the whole background of your conditioning; you reply accordingly, you think accordingly. The center of this background is the 'me' (the 'I' or ego) in the process of action.*

> *"So long as that background is not understood, so long as that thought process, that self which creates the problem, is not understood and put an*

end to, we are bound to have conflict, within and without, in thought, in emotion, in action..."

MEETING YOUR MONKEY MIND

To identify and actually get acquainted with your *"monkey mind"*, just follow these simple steps:

STEP 1:

Sit or lie down in a comfortable and relaxing position. The position you now have while reading this book will do. You can also adopt another position or a yoga pose (asana) if you like.

STEP 2:

Close your eyes and mentally say to yourself:

"I will now stop thinking for at least 30 seconds to prove that I am in control of my own mind."

STEP 3:

Mentally start counting from one to thirty without thinking.

STEP 4:

As you count, a series of *"involuntary thoughts"* are bound to

appear in your head. Each time this happens, stop counting, go back to number one, and start counting to thirty once again.

For example:

"One, two, three, four, five, where did I leave my car keys?, ooops!, one, two, three, four, five, six, I'm doing better this time!, Oh, no!, Start again!, one, two, three, four, five, etc."

STEP 5:

Repeat the process at least one or two minutes doing your best to stop thinking.

If you manage to count to thirty without thinking then you probably don't need to read this book (please return it and get a refund). But if you keep having thoughts regardless of your decision to stop thinking, this means you are not consciously in control of your mind.

But if you're consciously not in control of your own mind, then who is? Necessarily, the answer is your *"unconscious mind"*, which is constantly bombarding your head with new thoughts and mental chatter, always jumping from one thought to another and wandering without control, like a wild monkey...

Such is the unconscious nature of the "monkey mind" and its endless "mental chatter".

LESSON II

THE DREAM OF MAYA

"The phenomena of life may be likened unto a dream, a phantom; a bubble, a shadow, a glistening dew, or lightning flash, and as such they ought to be contemplated."

Prajna-Paramita

AN ANCIENT SAYING CLAIMS that *"we are what we think"*, to which the Bible wisely adds in Proverbs 4:23:

> *"Be careful how you think, for your*
> *life is shaped by your thoughts..."*

This capability of *"shaping our lives by our thoughts"* was brilliantly expressed by four hundred years ago by the 17th-century English poet John Milton in the pages of his *"Lost Paradise"*:

> *"The mind is its own place and in*
> *itself can make a Heaven of Hell, a Hell*
> *of Heaven."*

After tragically losing his sight at the age of 44 – just when he was starting to gain literary fame- his wife died as well as their one-year-old. All within four months!

John Milton was completely shattered!

Not only all he could see was darkness, but another form of darkness also fell upon him: the darkness of his own suffering and growing despair. For less reasons many have taken their own lives!

Driven by a lifelong quest for higher understanding, John Milton did not collapse. Accepting his fate he lived a life by many considered *"hell on earth"*. But soon learned from his tragedy and adopted new *"patterns of thinking and behaving"*. He virtually learned to *"see"* his cup half-filled instead of half-empty, turning darkness into light!

Not only did Milton soon remarry and father more children but he also hired a secretary, resumed his writing career and dictated his literary masterpiece, *"Lost Paradise"* which gave him worldwide fame in spite of his total blindness, literally *"making a heaven out of hell"*.

In his own words, regarding his personal tragedy and how he learned to cope with his loss of sight, he made the following confession in *"Lost Paradise"*:

> *"To be blind is not miserable; not to be*
> *able to bear blindness, that is miserable."*

Unfortunately, most people ignore they can determine their fate by the way they think and are constantly filling their heads with negative thoughts, paving the way for their own suffering, unhappiness, and confusion. And thus, unaware that their *"mental chatter"* is the only true cause of all their problems, worries, and sorrows, they sink deeper and deeper in their own negativity and end up creating their own private hell!

REPETITIVE NEGATIVE THINKING

Our negative thoughts alter our perception of the world and of ourselves.

This psychological phenomenon was first studied in the 1960s by the American psychiatrist and University of Pennsylvania professor Aaron T. Beck, also known as the Father of Cognitive Therapy.

Beck gave these altered perceptions the name of *"cognitive distortions"* and concluded they are exclusively sustained by the regular repetition of common negative thoughts such as:

"I feel so lonely!"

"I will never be happy".

"I need to be accepted."

"People always take advantage of me."

"I always have bad luck."

"I feel so depressed!"

"I am so angry"

"I cannot do anything right!"

"I will never succeed!"

"I will never be happy!"

"Nobody cares about me!"

"No one will ever love me!"

"No one understands me!

"Nobody can be trusted."

"I'm truly unattractive or ugly."

"I'm a loser!"

"He or she does not like or accept me."

"I'm so stupid!"

"I hate myself!"

"I can't stand it!"

YOUR PERSONAL IMAGE OF THE WORLD

If I ask you to please close your eyes and imagine a tree or a dog in your mind, you will most surely see an image of a tree or dog in your head.

This image in your mind, however, is only that: a mental image. It is not and it will never be a real tree or dog. But what most people almost never consider is that each time you imagine *"yourself"* or *"the world"*, whatever you see in your head is also the product of your own mental image of *"yourself"* or *"the world"*.

One thing is the *"real world"* in which we live; and another are the over seven billion different *"mental representations"* everyone on earth has of what he or she thinks is the *"real world"*.

Truth is, we all *"see"* the world in our own particular way, everyone with a different perspective or *"illusory idea of reality"*.

Proof of this is the fact that when you go through *"good times"* the world seems brighter and when you go through *"bad times"* it just doesn´t look so bright or not bright at all! For instance, the world seems bitter for those with thoughts of bitterness, sad for those with thoughts of sadness, unjust for those with thoughts of hatred and revenge, evil for those with thoughts of fear and suffering, etc. Psychologically, we all live in different realities!

This is why the olden sayings claim that:

"Each head is a world"

*"Everything **depends** on the **color** of the **glass** you look through. "*

"Beauty lies in the eye of the beholder"

THE DREAM OF ILLUSION

The process of creating our own interpretation of the world and of ourselves begins in our early childhood. And by the time we have reached adulthood, we are each truly living in our very own *"imaginary reality"* solely existing in our minds thus losing contact with *"real reality"*

A young man filled with thoughts of fear and failure, for example, will surely see the real world as difficult, threatening and unsatisfactory. He will experience this vividly, just like in a dream. And most probably, due to this he will always experience difficulties, threats and suffering in life.

This dream-like state of mind is capable of transforming our perception of reality before our very eyes. It is mostly evident in people with mental disorders, such as obsessives, maniacs, and psychopaths. But it is also present in practically every human being. In fact, everyone on this planet imagines a different *"world"* in their head, each imagining a different *"dream"*!

For thousands of years the ancient sages of India have known this as the *"dream of Maya or Illusion"*. In a nutshell, as the British philosopher and author James Allen expressed in 1902 in *"As Man Thinketh"*:

"Our thoughts either destroy or edify us."

MAYA'S "MAGIC SHOW"

Back in the 8th Century AD, the celebrated Hindu sage Adi Sankara compared in his legendary sermons the dream of Maya with *"a trick of a magician":*

> *"The world is like a dream full of attachments and aversions that seems real until the awakening...*

> *"As the magician is not at any time affected by the magical illusion produced by himself, because it is unreal, so is the highest Self not affected by the illusory visions of his dream, because they do not accompany the waking state and the state of dreamless sleep..."*

Sankara also announced how to free ourselves from this dream:

> *"Like the appearance of silver in mother of pearl, the world seems real until the Self, the underlying reality, is realized...*

> *"True to its deceptive nature, Maya is full of paradoxes. First of all, it is everywhere, even though it doesn't exist. The Mysterious One is nowhere if not in each person. Maya*

31

is not so omnipotent that we cannot control it
– and that is the key point."

"The pure truth of Atman, which is buried
under Maya, can be reached by meditation,
contemplation and other spiritual disciplines
such as a knower of Brahman may prescribe
-but never by subtle argument."

The cause of this illusory dream, as previously mentioned, are the repetitive thoughts of our *"monkey mind"*, that is, the endless mental chattering based on the idea of ourselves and of reality.

Because of this one of India´s greatest 20th century sages, Sri Ramana Maharshi (1879–1950) used to repeat that that *"the mind is Maya"*:

"The world should be considered like a
dream. Waking is long and a dream short;
other than this there is no difference.

"Just as waking happenings seem real
while awake, so do those in a dream while
dreaming.

"In dream the mind takes on another body. In both waking and dream states thoughts, names and forms occur simultaneously...

EXERCISE TWO

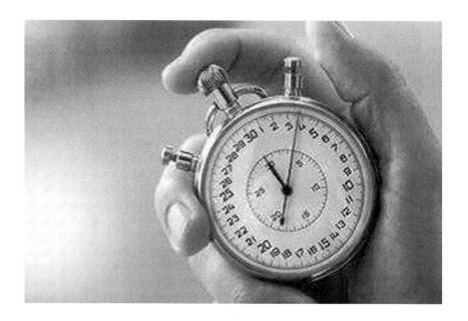

COUNTING YOUR THOUGHTS

OUR PERSONAL VIEW OF REALITY is shaped and nurtured by the nature and intensity of our unceasing *"internal dialogue"*, which is generated by what Krishnamurti calls our *"chattering mind"*, as we saw.

Modeled by this unceasing chatter we all create a *"parallel reality"* that only exists in our own imagination and that prevents us from experiencing reality as it truly is. Unfortunately, the more negative thoughts we incorporate in our chatter, the more the world affects us negatively - but only as long as we continue *"dreaming"* and refuse to *"awaken"*!

COUNTING YOUR THOUGHTS:

The following basic or preliminary exercise consists in counting the number of thoughts you have in one minute. For this practice I recommend the following:

> *A calculator.*

> *A stopwatch or something to keep track of time.*

> *Someone to assist you, basically so he or she can keep track of the time while you concentrate on the exercise. You can also take turns if you want.*

PART ONE OF THE EXERCISE:

(Estimated time: 1 or 2 minutes)

STEP 1:

Sit or lie down in a comfortable and relaxed position. The position you now have while reading this book will do. You can adopt a yoga pose or asana if you prefer.

STEP 2:

Close your eyes. You can also do this exercise keeping them open, but closing them avoids distractions and momentarily increases concentration.

STEP 3:

No matter what you're thinking when you close your eyes, that will be your *"Thought Number 1"*. For example you may be thinking *"I wonder what this exercise is all about"* or *"I'm hungry"* or *"Wow! I forgot to make a call!"* Whatever it may be, consider it your *"Thought Number 1"* and proceed to the next step.

STEP 4:

As soon as you identify your first thought, say mentally or out loud the word *"ONE"* (the number of the thought). This solely serves to keep count for the sake of this exercise and has no other practical purpose.

STEP 5:

After saying the number of your first thought, stop thinking about it. Simply don't get involved with it at this precise moment, leave it for later, and avoid participating an *"internal dialogue or conversation"*. Just let the thought go and jump to the next step.

STEP 6:

Be alert and wait for your next thought, which sooner or later will pop in your head. As soon as it appears, recognize it and keep count by saying either mentally or out loud the word *"TWO"* (the number of the second thought). Immediately after saying this, stop thinking about it, leave it for later, let it go.

STEP 7:

Repeat the process for exactly 60 seconds (a complete minute).

REMEMBER:

*Each time a new idea appears, repeat the process: recognize it, say its number and let it go.

*Don't get engaged in your thoughts during the exercise.

*Keep track of the number of thoughts you have counted by saying each number out loud.

*When the 60 seconds are up, write down the total number of thoughts you counted.

PART TWO: CALCULATING YOUR THOUGHT RATES

Take out your calculator, a piece of paper and a pencil or pen (You can also use your computer or laptop instead).

THOUGHTS PER MINUTE:

Write down the number of thoughts you had in 60 seconds (one minute). For example, the first time I did this exercise I had 25 thoughts per minute.

THOUGHTS PER HOUR:

Take the number of thoughts per minute and multiply it by 60.This will give you your THOUGHTS PER HOUR rate.

Suppose you had 25 thoughts, like I did:

25 x 60= 1,500 thoughts per hour!

THOUGHTS PER DAY:

To calculate your THOUGHTS PER DAY rate multiply your hourly rate times 24. That will give you your THOUGHTS PER DAY rate.

In my case: 1,500 x 24= 36,000 thoughts per day!

THOUGHTS PER YEAR:

Finally, multiply your daily rate by 365 and you will get your THOUGHTS PER YEAR rate.

In my case:

36,000 x 365= OVER 13 MILLION THOUGHTS PER YEAR!

(13,140,000 thoughts per year to be exact).

SOME QUESTIONS WORTH ASKING

You, as most people, also have thousands of thoughts each day and many millions each year. Now ask yourself:

*How many of these thoughts made you feel good?

*How many made you feel bad?

*How many were useful?

*How many were a waste of time?

*How many gave you inner peace?

*How many increased your sorrow, anger or stress?

*How many helped you attain spiritual progress?

*How many sank you deeper in the world of Illusion?

*How could you have made better use of your own thoughts?

The following pages will not only show you how basic meditation can help you make better use of your own thoughts but also how it can actually free you from the *"illusory world"* responsible from generating human problems, suffering, and unhappiness.

LESSON III

BASIC MANTRA MEDITATION

"You may control a mad elephant; You may shut the mouth of the bear and the tiger; Ride the lion and play with the cobra; By alchemy you may learn your livelihood; You may wander through the universe incognito; Make vassals of the gods; be ever youthful; You may walk in water and live in fire; But control of the mind is better and more difficult."

Paramahansa Yogananda

IN 1967 THE HINDU GURU Maharishi Mahesh Yogi (1918-2008), also known as *"The Guru of The Beatles"* gave a lecture on Transcendental Meditation (TM) at the London Hilton.

In the audience were George Harrison, John Lennon and Paul McCartney, in front-row seats. It was the first time the three Beatles personally met Maharishi and after the lecture they attended a 90-minute private audience with him. No one knows in detail what they talked, but they were fascinated with him and the following year the Beatles visited Maharishi's spiritual training camp in Rishikesh, India.

As George Harrison later recalled, he had read about Hindu *"mantra meditation"* and was really interested in learning how to practice it. And then one day he found out an Indian guru called Maharishi Mahesh Yogi was giving a lecture in London:

> *"I got the tickets. I was actually after a mantra. I had got to the point where I thought I would like to meditate; I'd read about it and I knew I needed a mantra - a password to get through to the other world. And, as we always seemed to do everything together, John and Paul came with me."*

It is said that TM helped the Beatles drop LSD. Truth is, by the mid-1970s TM had an estimated 600,000 practitioners. Among the celebrities that at one time or another have practiced TM, apart from the Beatles, are Shirley MacLaine, Mia Farrow, Mick Jagger, Brian Wilson, Donovan, Joe Namath, Jerry Seinfeld, Harrison Ford, Sting, Howard Stern, Hugh Jackman, Ellen DeGeneres, Richard Gere, Russell Brand, Oprah Winfrey, and Deepak Chopra.

In 1987, intrigued by Maharishi's fame, I read a few chapters of Maharishi's celebrated book *"The Science of Being and The Art of Living"* and decided to get my TM initiation. I was 30 years old (I am now 59). Sometime later, after paying the required fee and participating in a brief, private ceremony, my instructor gave me a "secret mantra" and taught me the basics of Maharishi's technique, guiding my first mantra meditation practice with great results.

This mantra was considered a *"sacred word" and I was told to never to reveal it before receiving the basic steps of the TM technique.*

What I most liked about using a mantra is that you don't really need to concentrate that much or control your thoughts while you meditate. You simply repeat the mantra mentally, effortlessly and easily. And every time a new thought arises you can simply return to repeating the mantra.

Mantra meditation, as I soon discovered, can make you experience relaxation and peace of mind. And with practice, it can also make you experience *"altered state of minds"* or *"trances"*, in which your mind is simply swept away!

THE THINKING GENIE AND THE POLE

Calming the "monkey mind" is a hard task. This is why in the ancient scrolls of the Bhagavad Gita, Lord Krishna warns his disciple Arjuna with these words:

> *"The mind is restless and very difficult to restrain. But I can assure you that the mind can be controlled by constant practice and non-attachment. For someone who is not self-controlled, this Yoga is difficult to attain, but not so for those who are self-controlled."*

The act of controlling or training the mind is illustrated by the following Hindu legend, in which a rich young man went to see a great guru seeking for advice for he had an urgent problem he could not solve.

"Please, tell me about your problem" the guru kindly asked the young man, noticing his evident despair.

"It´s hard to explain, master... I have a powerful genie under my command, he grants all my desires and is always eager to please me..."

"A genie, you say?" asked the guru, raising an eyebrow.

"Yes, Master, a genie who grants any desire with a simple snap of his fingers."

"Please tell me, if that genie of yours grants all your desires, then what is your problem?" the guru inquired.

"My problem is that my genie is extremely active and very impatient. He grants all my desires, like I said, but if I don't pay attention to him, he starts taking things back! As soon as he grants me one desire, he asks for the next! He never leaves me in peace! I truly don't know what to do!"

"Does the genie ever rest?" asked the guru.

"Never! And since he is so eager to please me, he is always by my side, waiting for my next command, even while I sleep! I no longer have a private life, Master! I can't even enjoy a quiet meal! Please help me! I don't know what to do!"

"Is this why you came to see me?" the guru asked raising an eyebrow after patiently hearing what the young man had to say.

"Yes, Master…"

"Then do not despair, for I have treated similar cases in the past…"

"You have?"

"Yes, and I have precisely what you need!"

It is said that after a long conversation, the guru bid farewell to the young man, who immediately returned to the luxurious palace the genie had created for him.

As expected, as soon as the young man opened the door and stepped into his palace, the genie appeared and after bowing before him he quickly said:

"Welcome back, Master! How can I serve you now?"

"Come with me, genie," said the young man, following the guru's advice, before stepping out of the building palace and walking to the garden that surrounded it.

"What is your wish, master?" the genie impatiently asked.

"I want you to create a long wooden pole for me and stick it in the middle of this garden".

"Oh, master, that shall be no problem!"

The genie snapped his fingers and instantaneously a long wooden pole appeared in the middle of the garden, stuck to the ground.

Immediately after doing this, the genie eagerly bowed before the young man and eagerly asked:

"Now tell me, master, how else can I serve you?"

"Now, genie," the young man said following the guru's advice, "I want you to climb up and down the pole, over and over again, as long as you resist".

"Your words are my command, master" the genie said before he started climbing up and down the pole.

And thus, the young man finally had some peace of mind!

That evening the guru went to see how the young man was doing and when they stepped into the garden they saw the genie placidly sleeping next to the pole.

"And so it is with the thinking genie every man has within his head" said the guru. "It is restless in its desire to satisfy our every desire, fragmenting our being. But the pole you have used is a priceless tool called a 'mantra'. And by repeating it over and over again, our restless mind is kept busy until it reaches stillness. And then our true Self fully enjoys the world!"

The "*thinking genie within the head*" mentioned by this Hindu legend represents the "*wandering monkey mind*" that never keeps still and is always jumping from thought to thought, from desire to desire.

And the act of climbing up and down the pole represents the ancient practice of mantra meditation, explained in the following pages.

MANTRA MEDITATION

As mentioned by the ancient Indian tale, mantra meditation is a common Hindu practice for calming the *"monkey mind"*, in this case is represented by the young man's pleasing and restless genie.

A mantra can be a sound, word, phrase or chant that is repeated over and over to stop our internal dialogue and generate inner calmness. Presently, thousands of mantras are used in different schools of Hinduism, Buddhism, Tibetan Buddhism, Jainism and Sikhism. And similar types of repetitious hymns, chants, and prayers are also found in Christianity, Zoroastrianism, and Taoism. However, it is believed that the first to use mantras in meditation were the ancient Hindu sages.

According to Hinduism, all mantras derive from *"the Father of all Sounds"*, represented by the word *"Om"* or *"Aum"*, which is popularly known as the *"universal mantra"*.

When meditating, Hindus repeat this mantra or another and try not to let their minds wander about and think about *"worldly things"*. They keep repeating the mantra over and over, until they become totally immersed in a state of silent inner-awareness and absolute present, in contact with their inner Self.

OM: THE UNIVERSAL MANTRA

Hindus believe the word Om represents the sacred name of God and that its original sound was produced when the universe was created.

According to Hindu mythology the word Om embodies the god Nirguna Brahman, also known as Nirgun, which represents the *"Supreme Reality Without Form or Qualities"*, also known as Paramatman (*"Superior Soul"* or *"Self Beyond"*) and Svayam Bhagavan (*"Without Form"* or *"The Absolute"*).

For thousands of years, Hindus have used the word Om as a basic chant or mantra for meditation. It is believed to be the highest of all mantras and it is believed that its continuous repetition creates a vibrating effect on human minds that naturally induces harmony, peace, and bliss. Also, its vibrating effect links up with the supreme energy of the Transcendental Self, the nameless, formless and ineffable essence of the universe.

MEDITATING ON THE WORD OM OR AUM

Hindus believe Om or Aum is the sacred name of Braham (God) and that its original sound was produced the exact moment our universe was created.

According to Hindu mythology the word Om embodies the god Nirguna Brahman, also known as Nirgun, which represents the "Supreme Reality Without Form or Qualities."

Nirguna Brahman is also known as Paramatman ("Superior Soul" or "Self Beyond") and Svayam Bhagavan ("Without Form" or "The Absolute").

When meditating, Hindus repeat the mantra and try not to let their minds wander and think about worldly things. They keep repeating the mantra until they become totally immersed in a state of inner awareness and absolute present. But for this they need to stop participating in their inner chat.

Pronouncing the word Om is said to create vibrations which link up with the supreme energy of Braham Nirguna or Paramatma, the formless life source of all creation in the universe.

For Hindus and Buddhists, Om is the primordial sound, the first breath of creation, the vibration that ensures existence. Om sign signifies God, Creation, and the Oneness of all creation.

Buddhists use it as *Om Mani Padme Hum.*

Christians and Jews use it as '*Amen*' to denote strong affirmation.

Our Muslim brothers and sisters use it as '*Aamin*'.

Sikhism is based on fundamental tenet of '*Ik Omkar*' or *One Om.*

In sum, there are many different ways of practicing Hindu meditation. And while some recommend sitting down in silence and adopting the lotus posture (padmasana) while placing the hands in front with the fingers in close touch with one another, others say the position of our bodies (asana) is not important and meditate while lying down, walking or even when doing their daily chores.

THREE WAYS OF REPEATING A MANTRA

According to the celebrated wandering Hindu monk Swami Vivekananda (1863-1902), there are three ways of repeating a mantra when meditating:

1: Verbal. The verbal or audible is the lowest effective, and the inaudible is the highest of all.

2: Semi-verbal. The semi-verbal is where only the lips move, but no sound is heard.

3: Mental. The inaudible repetition of the mantra is the most effective.

Vivekananda also mentions the two basic ways of purification, external and internal:

"The purification of the body by water, earth, or other materials, is the external purification, as bathing, etc. And purification of the mind by meditation is what is called internal purification. Both are necessary."

EXERCISE THREE

BASIC MANTRA MEDITATION

"There is no need to try to stop thinking because thoughts are a part of meditation. Even if the mind is filled with other thoughts while the mantra is going on, there is no conflict. Our concern is with the mantra, and if other thoughts are there along with it, we do not mind them and we don't try to remove them. We are not concerned with them, we innocently favor the mantra."

Maharishi Mahesh Yogi

MANTRA MEDITATION is an ancient Hindu practice used for thousands of years to calm the human mind, experience self-awareness, find inner peace and experience enlightenment. Now you can easily learn to practice mantra meditation by following the simple steps described in this exercise.

We will use the universal mantra, *"Om"* or *"Aum"* (which based on my own experience works fine).

STEP 1:

Sit or lie down in a comfortable and relaxing position. The position you now have while reading this book will do. You can also adopt another one or maybe a meditation or yoga pose.

STEP 2:

Close your eyes.

This will be your mantra: OM.

Begin repeating this word out loud a few times (you can use another mantra if you like, but I recommend starting out with the *"Father of All Mantras"*).

For example:

> *"Om, Om, Om, Om, Om, Om, Om,*
> *Om, Om, Om, etc."*

Consider the following:

*You can repeat it like normally or you can give it musicality and thus turn it into a *"one-syllable chant"*.

*You can repeat it slowly of fast, it depends on you. In any case, repeating it should be effortless and automatic...

As Maharishi Mahesh Yogi warns:

> *"One thing is very important, that we do not try to meditate. We do not try to keep the tempo of the mantra the same, nor do we try to change the tempo. And, we do not concentrate against thoughts we might have, or against noises we might hear.*

> *"We do not resist thoughts, we do not resist noise, we do not resist the mantra changing or disappearing, we do not resist anything. We take it as it comes. It is a very simple, natural, innocent process."*

STEP 3:

Continue repeating the mantra out loud a few more times, but each time you repeat it, gradually decrease the volume until you reach complete silence. However, during this step, do not stop moving your lips and tongue.

STEP 4:

Now, stop moving your lips and tongue and continue repeating the mantra mentally. Do it effortlessly. And every time a new thought arises, observe it but do not get involved (do not begin a new chatter). Simply accept the thought, let it go and return to the mantra discarding second thoughts...

For example:

> *"Om, Om, Om, Om, Gosh, I'm thirsty! Hey! I'm not repeating the mantra! Om, Om, Om, Om..."*

STEP 5:

Gradually, instead of repeating it mentally, try to *"hear its repetition as a faint idea within your mind"*.

> *"Om, Om, Om, Om, Om, Om, Om..."*

Regarding this step of the practice, Maharishi Mahesh Yogi describes the following:

> *"Mental repetition is not a clear pronunciation. It is just a faint idea. We don't try to make a rhythm of the mantra. We don't try to control thoughts. We do not wish that thoughts should not come. If a thought comes, we*

do not try to push it out. We don't feel sorry about it.

"When a thought comes, the mind is completely absorbed in the though... When we become aware that we are not thinking the mantra, then we quietly come back to the mantra.

"Very easily we think the mantra and if at any moment we feel that we are forgetting it, we should not try to persist in repeating it. Only very easily we start and take it as it comes and do not hold the mantra if it tends to slip away...

"The mantra may change in different ways. It can get faster or slower, louder or softer, clearer or fainter. Its pronunciation may change, lengthen or shorten or even may appear to be distorted or it may not appear to change at all. In every case, we take it as it comes, neither anticipating nor resisting change, just simple innocence."

DON´T JUDGE YOUR THOUGHTS

As you repeat the mantra, many thoughts are bound to arise even if you do your best to stop thinking. Some of these thoughts will seem to be more important than others and may momentarily absorb you and make you stop repeating the mantra.

The rule of thumb is:

No matter how important they seem, don´t judge or evaluate your thoughts! Important or not, give them all the same treatment: That is, recognize them, understand what they mean and then, without judging them, "*release them*" and return to the mantra.

The moment you give a thought or idea too much importance, it will end up absorbing you and, most probably, you will begin a new "*internal dialogue*" or "*monologue*" within your head... and thus you will stop repeating the mantra!

Therefore, no matter what, the key is to not give your thoughts any importance whatsoever. Don´t kick them out of your head, but don´t become absorbed by them either. Simply, don´t judge or evaluate them, and realize that no single thought is more important than another, for will all necessarily have to wait for later (for after you meditate).

LESSON IV

THE SILENT OBSERVER

"The meditative mind is seeing, watching, listening, without the word, without comment, without opinion, attentive to the movement of life in all its relationships throughout the day..."

Jiddu Krishnamurti

AFTER LEARNING TO REPEAT YOUR MANTRA and releasing your thoughts, the next step consists in directing your attention to "the thinker" (monkey-mind) by adopting the state of *"the Silent Observer or Self"* differentiating yourself from your own thoughts.

As we will see, the chattering mind and the Silent Observer are two completely different *"actors"* within our heads. And recognizing their differences is the basis of the first step of what Hindus call *"Self-knowledge"*.

But what is Self-knowledge?

Basically, the knowledge that we are not *"the thinker"* but the *"Silent Witness"*, that is, our True Inner Self. This is why the ancient masters of Hinduism divided the study of Self-knowledge in two separate branches (although they also admit that in essence they are truly one):

> *The knowledge of the animal self or ego (our psychological "I", the thinker or chattering monkey-mind)*

> *The knowledge of the true Self or soul, (our transcendental "I", true Self or Silent Observer)*

THE SLAVE OF YOUR MIND

According to Eckhart Tolle, if you cannot control your mind chatter, then the mind is actually controlling you!

And that´s a problem you can´t afford!

The reason for not being able to control our minds is that most people become unconsciously identified with their "inner voice" and are "slaves" of their own thoughts, beliefs, values, and desires.

And as Eckhart states, the only way to realize that you are a slave of your own mind and free yourself from its influence is by becoming an "observing intelligence".

This means becoming the Observer, which is the basic goal of this second level of instruction.

Only by becoming Observer you will "see" who you really are.

This is why all the ancient wise men highlighted the importance of the maxim inscribed in the Temple of Apollo at Delphi: *"Know thyself"*.

That´s basically it.

You really need to know yourself!

And the only way to do this, as you will see in the following lessons, is through Self-knowledge, that is, by observing your thoughts, slowing down your "inner chatter", and learning to experience "inner stillness".

No one else can do this for you.

Only you can!

KNOWLEDGE OF OUR TRUE SELF

According to Hinduism, our true Self lies beyond time, space and phenomena. It is also identified with God or the Ultimate Reality, which;

> *Constitutes the essence of the Transcendental Reality.*

> *Has no form. It has no name.*

> *Is limitless. It is not bound. It is beyond space and time.*

> *Is the ineffable Being that sustains the universe.*

> *Transcends speech and therefore cannot be described.*

> *Is our inner-Self , a subjective awareness of "I am".*

> *Is our real form (nija-swarupa).*

Dwells in the center of our heart.

The ego, on the other hand, has nothing to do with our true nature.

We just said that our true Self is also associated with God.

But what is God?

To answer this question let's take a quick glance at seven of the world's main religions and what they have to say regarding this matter:

CHRISTIANITY:

In the 13th century the Italian friar and theologian, Saint Thomas Aquinas (1225-1274), also known as *"Doctor Angelicus"*, concluded in his *"Compendium of Theology"* that the divine essence of God cannot be defined:

> *"Since our intellect does not adequately grasp the divine essence in any of the conceptions which the names applied to God signify, the definitions of these terms cannot define what is in God. That is, any definition we might formulate of the divine wisdom would not be a*

definition of the divine power, and so on regarding other attributes.

"The same is clear for another reason. A definition is made up of genus and specific differences, for what is properly defined is the species. But we have shown that the divine essence is not included under any genus or species. Therefore it cannot be defined."

Concerning the transcendental experience of *"Oneness with God"*, in the 14th century the German mystic and Dominican monk known as Meister Eckhart (1260-1327), proclaimed that *"the Divine Nature is One"* and that we are all *"both One and the same One as God's Nature"*:

"God is pure Oneness, being free of any accretive multiplicity of distinction even at a conceptual level."

HINDUISM:

Regarding God, over a century ago Vivekananda explained the traditional view of Hinduism as follows:

"According to the Advaita philosophy, there is only one thing Real in the universe, which it calls Brahman (God or

the Ultimate Reality)...everything else is unreal, manifested and manufactured out of Brahman by the power of Maya (Illusion)... To reach back to that Brahman is our goal.

"We are, each one of us, that Brahman, that Reality, plus this Maya. But if we can get rid of this Maya or ignorance, then we become what we really are... That what is called the Atman (the Supreme Soul), which is our true Self."

BUDDHISM:

Buddha stated that the question of God is not useful and does not lead to the end of suffering. However, he mentioned an Eternal Dharma or Supreme Reality, which he also called Nirvana, Eternity, Emptiness, Suchness, Truth, Dharmadhatu (Realm of Dharma), Sameness, Non-Duality (Oneness), the Imperishable, and the All-Knowing, among other denominations.

Buddha claimed that *"Oneness"* is *"the spiritually charged nature of everything that is"*. As a Zen Buddhism old saying states: *"Oneness is everything, everything is oneness."*

ISLAM (SUFISM):

The mystical branch of Islam known as Sufism took formal shape in Persia in the early Middle Ages based on the Islamic *"doctrine of Oneness"* and the belief that *"in everything that exists"* is Allah or God, also known as *"The Formless"*, *"The Colorless"*, and *"The One Real Being Which Underlies All Phenomena"*, among other denominations.

According to Sufism, the experience of God or Illumination is produced *"when the individual self is lost"* and *"the Universal Self is found"*.

TAOISM:

Taoism (Daoism) is considered China's oldest religion and took its definite form around the 6th century B.C., when the Chinese master Lao Tzu wrote his celebrated spiritual book, the *"Tao Te Ching"*.

As Lao Tzu stated, the only Truth is the eternal Tao, which cannot be described for *"the Tao that can be mentioned is not the eternal Tao"*. It is considered the *"mystery of mysteries"* as well as *"the door to all wonders!"* It is not a thing or a being, nevertheless all things and beings derive from it. It has no substance; however it gives rise to all substances. It is not nothing, but is not something either. There is no explanation. The Tao is simply the inexpressible, the ineffable.

SIKHISM:

Also from India and derived from Hinduism and Islam, Sikhism is a religion founded during the 15th century by the spiritual leader Guru Nanak (1469-1539), who at the age of thirty, he declared:

> *"There is neither Hindu nor Muslim, so whose path shall I follow? I shall follow God's path! God is neither Hindu nor Muslim. And the path which I follow is God's!"*

Guru Nanak spread a simple message contained at the beginning of the Sikh holy book, the Guru Granth Sahib:

> *"There is but One God, His name is Truth, He is the Creator, He fears none, He is without hate, He never dies, He is beyond the cycle of births and death, He is self-illuminated, He is realized by the kindness of the True Guru. He was True in the beginning, He was True when the ages commenced and has ever been True, He is also True now."*

According to the Guru Granth Sahib, God is indescribable, inestimable, indubitable, intangible, imperishable, immutable, immortal, immaculate, immanent, formless, timeless, ageless, omnipresent, and creator of all.

JUDAISM:

Judaism has two different levels of spiritual teachings. The first level is based on studying the Bible, which contains the public teachings of Judaism. A second level, however, is contained in the Kabbalah, the *"hidden"* or **"secret" teachings** needed to interpret the Bible correctly.

According to the precepts of the Kabbalah, passed down by rabbinical oral tradition for thousands of years, God cannot be defined nor categorized, as the 16th century Kabbalistic master Rabbi Moshe Cordovero (1522-1570) explained:

> *"An impoverished person thinks that God is an old man with white hair, sitting on a wondrous throne of fire that glitters with countless sparks, as the Bible states: "The Ancient-of-Days sits, the hair on his head like clean fleece, his throne–flames of fire." Imagining this and similar fantasies, the fool corporatizes God. He falls into one of the traps that destroy faith. His awe of God is limited by his imagination. But if you are enlightened, you know God's oneness; you know that the divine is devoid of bodily categories - these can never be applied to God."*

TRUE SELF AND THE DREAM OF MAYA

To metaphorically describe how the dream of Maya hides our True Self from us, blinding us and making us believe we are someone we are not, Vivekananda used to mention the following ancient tale:

> *It is said that the king of the gods, the powerful Indra, Lord of Heaven, woke up one morning being a pig.*
>
> *Nobody could explain it! But there he was, wallowing in the mud; with a she-pig and a lot of baby pigs. And worst of all ...he was very happy!*
>
> *When the gods saw his situation, they immediately approached him and said:*
>
> *"Oh, Lord Indra! You are the king of the gods and have them under your command! Why are you here?"*
>
> *And Indra raised his pig face and replied:*
>
> *"Never mind; don't worry about me. I'm all right here. I do not care for heaven*

while I have this sow and these little pigs."

The poor gods were at their wits' end.

Not knowing what else to do, after a time they decided to slay all the pigs one after another.

When all the pigs were dead, Lord Indra began to weep and mourn intensely.

Then the gods ripped his pig-body open and he came out of it, and began to laugh when he realized what a hideous dream he had had. He, the king of the gods, to have become a pig, and to think that that pig-life was the only life!

Not only so, but to have wanted the whole universe to come into the pig-life!

The Purusha, when it identifies itself with nature, forgets that it is pure and infinite.

The Purusha does not love, it is love itself. It does not exist, it is existence itself.

The Soul does not know, It is knowledge itself.

OUR TRUE SELF IS SPIRIT

The celebrated Hindu sage Sri Ramana Maharshi was only sixteen when he casually *"discovered"* meditation and attained spiritual enlightenment. Back then he was known as Venkataraman and lived with his family in his home town, Madurai. He had never shown any special interest in spirituality and made his transcendental *"discovery"* rather innocently, without any preparation, spiritual guidelines nor sacred readings:

"It was about six weeks before I left Madurai for good that the great change in my life took place. It was so sudden. One day I sat up alone on the first floor of my uncle's house. I was in my usual health. I seldom had any illness. I was a heavy sleeper...

"So, on that day as I sat alone there was nothing wrong with my health. But a sudden and unmistakable fear of death seized me. I felt I was going to die.

"Why I should have felt so cannot now be explained by anything felt in my body.

Nor could I explain it to myself then. I did not, however, trouble myself to discover if the fear was well grounded. I felt 'I was going to die,' and at once set about thinking out what I should do.

"I did not care to consult doctors or elders or even friends. I felt I had to solve the problem myself then and there. The shock of fear of death made me at once introspective, or 'introverted'.

"I said to myself mentally -without uttering the words: 'Now, death has come. What does it mean? What is it that is dying? This body dies.'

"I at once dramatized the scene of death. I extended my limbs and held them rigid as though rigor-mortis had set in. I imitated a corpse to lend an air of reality to my further investigation. I held my breath and kept my mouth closed, pressing the lips tightly together so that no sound might escape. Let not the word 'I' or any other word be uttered!

"I said to myself: 'Well then, this body is dead. It will be carried stiff to the burning ground and there burnt and reduced to ashes. But with the death of this body, am 'I' dead? Is the body 'I'? This body is silent and inert. But I feel the full force of my personality and even the sound 'I' within myself, - apart from the body. So 'I' am a spirit, a thing transcending the body. The material body dies, but the spirit transcending it cannot be touched by death. I am therefore the deathless spirit!

"All this was not a mere intellectual process, but flashed before me vividly as living truth, something which I perceived immediately, without any argument almost..."

The *"deathless spirit"* Ramana identified himself with during his experience was his true Self.

EXERCISE FOUR

BECOMING THE SILENT WITNESS

LEARNING TO BECOME THE *"SILENT WITNESS"* and ceasing to identify with *"the thinker"* is a vital step you must take if you hope to fully experience the peaceful and healing benefits of meditation.

Repeating the mantra is vital, of course, but it is not enough.

The next step of this ancient Self-Awareness practice consists in learning how to identify and differentiate *"the thinker"* from *"the silent witness"*, which jointly participate in our mind.

To achieve this, just follow these basic and simple steps:

STEP 1:

Sit or lie down in a comfortable and relaxing position. The position you now have while reading this book will do or a meditation or yoga pose if you like.

STEP 2:

Close your eyes. Start repeating the mantra (first out loud and then mentally). As soon as a thought arises, observe it without judging it, simply let it be before *"releasing it"* and return to the mantra, as you learned to do in the last exercises.

STEP 3:

Try to be mentally quiet and alert as you continue repeating the mantra. Simply be aware and wait for your next thought before repeating the process over and over for one or two minutes.

STEP 4:

As you repeat the mantra and observe your thoughts, try to identify the two distinctive *"players"* participating within your head:

1: The voice of your thoughts.

2: The Silent Witness.

Are you the thoughts that are going through your head or the witness of these thoughts as they are going through your head?

The thoughts going through your head come from the voice of the ego, your false self, whereas your true conscience remains with the Silent Witness, which in fact is your true Self.

STEP 5:

Avoid engaging yourself with your thoughts, leave them for later and release them, one by one... And as you repeat the process continue experiencing the separation between the *"voice in your head"* (which bases its workings on logic, verbal language and *"what is expected"*) and the Silent Witness (you as the non-judging observer).

Ceasing to identify yourself with the ego is vital to fully identify yourself with the Silent Observer, which in fact constitutes your true Self.

LESSON V

THE SILENT GAP

"Remaining quiet is what is called wisdom-insight. To remain quiet is to resolve the mind in the Self..."

Ramana Maharshi

ONCE YOU RECOGNIZE the stream of thoughts that is unceasingly created by *"the thinker"* and begin to identify yourself with the non-judgmental *"silent witness"*, the next step consists in learning to identify and experience *"the silent gaps between thoughts"*.

Stressing the value of inner silence, the 20th-century Hindu sage Ramana Maharshi stated:

> *"Remaining quiet is what is called wisdom-insight. To remain quiet is to resolve the mind in the Self..."*

Similarly, seven centuries ago the German Dominican monk and mystic Meister Eckhart (1260-1327) said:

> *"There is a huge silence inside each of us that beckons us into itself, and the recovery of our own silence can begin to teach us the language of Heaven.*
>
> *"The unity (of God) is un-necessitous; it has no need of speech, but subsists alone in unbroken silence."*

After learning to establish yourself as the Observer and to slow down and interrupt your *"inner chat"* through mental practice, you will begin to experience a growing number of silent *"gaps of "inner stillness"* between one thought and the next.

The more you observe these gaps, the more you will begin to experience a *"present without thoughts"* that exists beyond the illusory nature of human thinking. But to do this you first need to develop your "inner eye": The Eye of the Observer, of your Higher Self.

Mystics of various spiritual traditions have mentioned a *"divine light"* that can only be perceived by the *"eye of the soul"* and that allows us to momentarily transcend reality. Among these stands the early Christian mystic and theologian Saint Augustine (354-430 AD), who in the early days of the Church described a mystic state as follows:

> *"And with the eye of my soul I saw above*
> *the same eye of my soul, above my mind, the*
> *Unchangeable Light ... He who knows the*
> *truth knows that light: and he that knows it*
> *knows Eternity."*

Fact is, this light perpetually shines within us but we have created an imaginary world that hides it, a world of illusion known by the ancient sages of India as the world of Maya or Illusion, the world of our false *"I"* or *"ego"*.

What is the *"ego"*?

One of the best definitions I've found belongs to the celebrated American psychiatrist and author Dr. Wayne Dyer (1940-2015), who a few years before passing away expressed the following in one of his remarkable blogposts:

> *"No one has ever seen the face of ego. It is like a ghost that we accept as a controlling influence in our lives. I look upon the ego as nothing more than an idea that each of us has about ourselves. The ego is only an illusion, but a very influential one. Letting the ego-illusion become your identity can prevent you from knowing your true self. Ego, the false idea of believing that you are what you have or what you do, is a backwards way of assessing and living life...*
>
> *"The ego-idea has been with us ever since we began to think. It sends us false messages about our true nature. It leads us to make assumptions about what will make us happy and we end up frustrated. It pushes us to promote our self-importance while we yearn for a deeper and richer life experience. It causes us to fall into the void of self-absorption again and again, not knowing that we need only shed the false idea of who we are.*

"Our true self is eternal. It is the God force within us. The way of our higher self is to reflect our inner reality rather than the outer illusion. The description given by Sogyal Rinpoche in "The Tibetan Book of Living and Dying" is a wonderful explanation of this discovery: 'Two people have been living in you all of your life. One is the ego, garrulous, demanding, hysterical, calculating; the other is the hidden spiritual being, whose still voice of wisdom you have only rarely heard or attended to.' He refers to this hidden spiritual being as our wise guide.

"When we learn to transcend the illusions sponsored by the ego, we can access this wise guide. We can invite in the higher aspects of ourselves to function in their natural, loving, and integrated design.

Source: http://www.drwaynedyer.com/blog/the-ego-illusion/

FALSE PERCEPTION OF YOURSELF

According to Eckhart Tolle, *"as you grow up, you form a mental image of which you are, based on your personal and cultural conditioning. We may call this phantom self the ego."*

Eckhart claims that your *"ego"* or *"rational mind"* needs constant thinking to exist and that people become addicted to thinking because they are identified with their erroneous *"sense of self"*.

Building your ego is like building a castle in your imagination.

The more you think about it, the more details you will imagine and the stronger your mental image of the castle will be. Only that in the case of your imaginary self-image the castle is shaped after you!

No matter what you think about yourself, your *"mental image of who you are"* is necessarily a supposition, a speculation, an imaginary picture that you have created and that only exists in your head!

It is only an illusion!

THE FALSE MATRIX OF THE EGO

In the celebrated film *Matrix* (1999), Thomas A. Anderson is a skillful computer expert living two lives: By day he is a common computer programmer. But by night he is a secret hacker known as Neo.

Neo is a rebel. He has always questioned his present. He is unsatisfied with his reality. He definitely needs a change. But he never imagined that soon he would find out that everything he had lived in his life was only a dream!

A vain illusion just like Nerada's!

This is how Neo´s amazing and futuristic story begins:

Neo is contacted by Morpheus, a legendary computer hacker and known terrorist. Neo has heard a lot about him. He has always secretly admired him as his superior in age, experience, and wisdom. But he knows Morpheus only means trouble!

Morpheus surprises Neo by suddenly asking him:

"Have you ever had a dream, Neo, that you were so sure was real? What if you were unable to wake from that dream? How would you know the difference between the dream-world and the real world?"

Morpheus then tells Neo the world as they know it is only an illusory dream that veils another world.

But Neo refuses to believe it!

To convince him, Morpheus tells him what he calls "the truth":

The "illusion of this world" is a perpetual dream artificially created by an enslaving machine called The Matrix, which feeds on human bio-electricity.

"The Matrix is a computer-generated dream-world built to keep us under control in order to change a human being into this," Morpheus said, holding up a Duracell battery.

"No!" Neo exclaimed shaking his head in denial. "I don't believe it! It's not possible!

"The Matrix is everywhere" Morpheus continued saying. "It is all around us. Even now, in this very room. You can see it when you look out your window or when you turn on your television. You can feel it when you go to work... when you go to church... when you pay your taxes. It is the world that has been pulled over your eyes to blind you from the truth."

"What truth?" asks Neo.

"That you are a slave, Neo. Like everyone else you were born into bondage. Into a prison that you cannot taste or see or touch. A prison for your mind."

* * *

Did you notice any similarities between Matrix and the world of Maya? For the purpose of this lesson, I would like to point out only two:

*The false Neo (trapped in the Illusion of the Matrix) can be compared with our "illusory self" or ego.

*The real Neo (free from the Illusion of the Matrix) can be compared with our natural or true Self.

Having said that, the moral of the story seems quite clear:

Only through Self-knowledge we can escape from the world of Illusion and transcend from ego to Self.

EXERCISE FIVE

EXPERIENCING THE SILENT GAP

AS MENTIONED EARLIER our endless thinking is constantly generating an *"internal dialogue"* within our heads, generating thousands of thoughts per day that perpetually give shape to our *"illusory or imaginary personal world"*. However, you can lean to stop this endless mental dialogue by meditating regularly and focusing on the brief moment or gap of silence that exists between one thought and another, in which you can experience inner stillness.

Whenever you pay attention to these gaps, according to Eckhart Tolle:

> *"Awareness of 'something' becomes just awareness. The formless dimension of pure*

*consciousness arises from within you and
replaces identification with form."*

To begin to see beyond the veil of illusion that blinds us all it takes is learning how to still your mental chatter and begin to experience these silent gaps, as the following exercise teaches.

Just follow these steps:

STEP 1:

Sit or lie down in a comfortable and relaxing position. The position you now have while reading this book will do or a meditation or yoga pose if you like.

STEP 2:

Close your eyes. Start by repeating the mantra (first out loud and then mentally) and by becoming the Silent Witness. As soon as a new thought arises, observe and understand what it means, without judging it, simply *"let it be"* before *"releasing it"* and then return to repeating the mantra, as you learned to do in the last exercises.

STEP 3:

Try to be mentally alert as you continue repeating the mantra. And while you wait for your next thought concentrate on the *"silent gap"* between thoughts. Be aware: Before your new thought arrives, you will experience a brief blank space that may only last a brief instant, so pay attention.

In his book "*Stillness Speaks*" Eckhart Tolle recommends:

> "*Pay attention to the gap, the gap between two thoughts, the brief, silent space between words in a conversation, between the notes of a piano or flute, or the gap between the in-breath and the out-breath.*

> "*When you pay attention to those gaps, awareness of 'something' becomes just awareness. The formless dimension of pure consciousness arises from within you and replaces identification with form.*"

He also explains in "*A New Earth*":

> "*You don't need to be concerned with the duration of those gaps. A few seconds is good enough. Gradually, they will lengthen themselves, without any effort on your part.*

> "*More importantly than their length is to bring them in frequently so that your daily activities and your stream of thinking become interspersed with space.*"

Each time a new thought arises, as it inevitably will, don't think anything else about it, don't judge it and don't try to push it away. Instead of doing this, simply understand its meaning, release it and return to your mantra.

If you pay attention you will experience brief gaps of pure awareness and silence. Initially the experience may only last a second or even brief microseconds, so keep your *"inner eye"* wide open.

Regarding the benefits of this spiritual practice, Eckhart Tolle points out the following in *"The Power of Now"*:

> *"When a thought subsides, you experience a discontinuity in the mental stream —a gap of no-mind. At first, the gaps will be short, a few seconds perhaps, but gradually they will become longer. When these gaps occur, you feel a certain stillness and peace inside you.*

> *"This is the beginning of your natural state of felt oneness with Being, which is usually obscured by the mind. With practice, the sense of stillness and peace will deepen. In fact, there is no end to its depth. You will also feel a subtle emanation of joy arising from deep within: the joy of Being."*

STEP 4:

Repeat the process one or two minutes. Concentrate on experiencing longer gaps. Don't judge your thoughts or start a mental dialogue. Simply observe and release them while repeating the mantra and concentrating on the silent gaps between thoughts.

LESSON VI

EXPERIENCING INNER PEACE NOW!

"When the mind is relaxed, no longer making an effort, when it is quiet for just a few seconds, then the problem reveals itself and it is solved."

Ramana Maharshi

A. J.　P A R R

YOU CAN EXPERIENCE INNER SILENCE by doing the exercises contained in this book and reinforcing it through meditating regularly. The repeated experience of these *"silent gaps"* will be your passport to gradual spiritual progress and experiencing inner peace.

You can also begin to experience this today by doing all the exercises and learning to apply your mantra in *"stressful situations"*, when it is imperative to keep calm. And you should also repeat the mantra whenever you have *"time to kill"*, instead of losing yourself in your own thoughts in those moments.

When you´re driving to work, for example, or while walking or waiting for someone or something are great times to repeat the mantra and meditate.

Starting today, taking these measures will certainly help you stop your *"internal dialogue"*, especially in *"times of trouble"*, that is, whenever you find yourself in any of the following situations:

> **Excessively "tied up" in your own thoughts and can´t stop thinking.*

> **Excessively stressed with something, someone or yourself.*

> **Excessively worried about someone, something or yourself.*

Excessively angry at someone, something or yourself.

Excessively sad about someone, something or yourself.

Excessively excited about something, someone, or yourself.

Excessively confused about someone, something, or yourself.

Excessively afraid of someone or something.

Excessively insomniac.

Excessively discouraged.

Excessively depressed.

Excessively nervous.

In sum, starting today you can use your mantra to actually help you *ANY TIME YOU NEED TO STOP THINKING NEGATIVELY.*

And you can mentally repeat the mantra anywhere and anytime, including when you´re:

Walking

Driving

Going up or down stairs.

In the elevator.

In the bus, subway or cab.

Waiting in line.

Waiting for someone or something.

Taking a break at work without leaving your desk.

Eating.

Taking a bath.

Going to the bathroom.

Having sex.

Doing your daily activities.

DIFFERENT WAYS OF MEDITATING

People interested in learning Hindu meditation often ask: *"How should I meditate? Do I need to sit with my back straight or can I lie down? Should I close my eyes or can I leave them open? Do I necessarily have to repeat a mantra or a chant? If not, what should I do?"*

Truth is, there are many ways of practicing meditation, apart from the method described by Krishna in the Bhagavad Gita.

These go from mentally visualizing the form of God of your choice, concentrating on your inner sound and light, meditating on sacred writings and teachings, or repeating specific mantras or chants.

One of the most common devotional practices in India is known as *"the repetition of God's name"*, a specific form of meditation that serves to center our attention on the Lord using the name and form or our choice. Repeating the name is known as *"nama"* and meditating on the form is known as *"rupa"*.

Another way of meditating was often recommended by Swami Sivananda and is based on listening to our *"inner sounds"*, which consists in closing both ears with our index fingers, a technique known as Laya-Yoga.

Some techniques are based on different forms of mental visualizations, while others never use visualizations at all. Other techniques are based on working with the body (*Hatha Yoga*) or the breath (*pranayama*).

There are those who meditate through the use of music and chanting, which soothes the anxious mind. For example, the practice of the Hare Krishna Movement depends on the repeated chanting of Krishna's Maha Mantra (Great Mantra), first mentioned in the Kali-Santarana Upanishad:

"Hare Rama, Hare Rama

Rama Rama, Hare Hare

Hare Krsna, Hare Krsna

Krsna Krsna, Hare Hare."

Another mantra widely used in India is known as the "Gayatri mantra". Considered as Vedasara (*"the essence of the Vedas"*), this sacred mantra evidences the unity that underlies manifoldness in creation and it is through the recognition of this unity that we can understand multiplicity:

Om Bhur Buvaha Suvaha

Thath Savithur Varenyam

Bhargo Devasya Dheemahi

Dhiyo Yonaha Prachodayath

Although hundreds of different mantras are used in Hinduism, it is said that they all derive from *"the Father of all Sounds"*, represented by the word Om or Aum, known as the universal mantra. Hindus believe this is the sacred name of Nirguna Braham or Paramatman (God or the Superior Self) and that its original sound was produced the moment our universe was created.

INNER TRANSFORMATION

The Path of Self-Knowledge always leads to inner transformation.

Regarding when this transformation actually takes place, Krishnamurti sustained the following in *"The First and Last Freedom"*:

> *"Transformation is in the future, can never be in the future. It can only be now, from moment to moment... When you see that something is false, that false thing drops away...*
>
> *"As we are surrounded by so much that is false, perceiving the falseness from moment to moment is transformation.*

EXERCISE SIX

FACING STRESSFUL SITUATIONS

AMONG ITS IMMEDIATE APPLICATIONS, meditation can help you find the best way to face *"stressful situations"* and avoid excessive thinking by applying three simple steps:

STEP 1:

Ask yourself who is having these thoughts.

The obvious answer is *"I am having these thoughts"*. But, as we have seen, the *"I"* represents our false self, the ego, which is only an illusion, a product of Maya!

And if the *"I"* is an illusion then everything I presently think and believe about my alleged *"stressful situation"* must also be an illusion! Therefore, my excessive thinking is the only true source of all my problems!

This revealing technique known as *"I Am Meditation"* was first described by Ramana Maharshi in a sermon delivered in 1902 and included in *"The Teachings of Bhagavan Sri Ramana Maharshi"*, transcribed from his sermons by one of his many dear disciples:

> *"How will the mind become still? By the inquiry 'Who am I?'. The thought 'who am I?' will destroy all other thoughts, and like the stick used for stirring the burning pyre, it will itself in the end get destroyed. Then, there will arise Self-realization.*

> *"How can one constantly hold on to the thought 'Who am I?' When other thoughts arise, one should not pursue them, but should inquire: 'Who is having these thoughts?'*

STEP 2:

Immediately begin to repeat the mantra in your head, no matter what you're doing, become the Silent Witness and try to observe your own thinking.

Regarding the attitude you should adopt in these cases, Krishnamurti stated the following:

> *"The meditative mind is seeing, watching, listening, without the word, without comment, without opinion, attentive to the movement of life in all its relationships throughout the day... When the mind is relaxed, no longer making an effort, when it is quiet for just a few seconds, then the problem reveals itself and it is solved.*
>
> *"That happens when the mind is still, in the interval between two thoughts, between two responses. In that state of mind, understanding comes..."*

STEP 3:

Apply the technique of *"releasing your thoughts"* as you repeat the mantra, to avoid engaging yourself in negative thinking. Observe your thoughts, release them, and try to experience the relaxing silence and inner peace of the *"gaps"* between thoughts.

Regarding this last step, Ramana Maharshi expressed:

> *"It does not matter how many thoughts arise. As each thought arises, one should inquire with diligence, 'Who is having these thoughts?' The answer that would emerge would be 'To me'.*

> *"Therefore, if one inquires 'Who am I?', the mind will go back to its source; and the thought that arose will become quiescent. With repeated practice in this manner, the mind will develop the skill to stay in its source..."*

Evidently, you can apply these three steps to calm your mind anytime and anywhere. And the more you apply them the smoother the whole process will get, accelerating your inner transformation.

AVOIDING NEGATIVE THOUGHTS

This three-step technique can be extremely useful whenever you find yourself facing trouble or feel extremely sad, nervous, worried or enraged.

Remember the ancient Chinese Proverbs when you apply these steps:

> *"You cannot prevent the birds of sorrow from flying over your head, but you can*

prevent them from building nests in your hair."

This means that you cannot avoid having negative thoughts of sadness, trouble, worry, regret, confusion, guilt and even rage every now and then. The important thing is to learn to *"release"* these negative thoughts as soon as you identify them and thus prevent them from becoming the central theme of your *"inner chatter"*, preventing these *"birds of sorrow"* from *"building nests in your hair"*.

In sum, you cannot avoid having negative thoughts but you can choose *"not to listen"*, as the XIV Dalai Lama expressed:

> *"Even the high Lamas of Tibet experience the ceaseless stream of thoughts running through our minds. The only difference is, we don't listen."*

Don't forget the more you use the techniques described in this book the more they will help you and the more you will stop worrying!

DON'T RESIST, SIMPLY SURRENDER

If you're experiencing intense depression, suffering, or are constantly worried about something you cannot possibly change, then humbly accept your reality, hand all your troubles to God, fate, or destiny, and *"surrender"* to the present moment.

Regarding this inner attitude or state of mind Eckhart Tolle states in *"The Power of Now"*:

> *"Surrender is a purely inner phenomenon.*
> *It does not mean that on the outer level you*
> *cannot take action and change the situation. In*
> *fact, it is not the overall situation that you*
> *need to accept when you surrender, but just*
> *the tiny segment called the Now..."*

He adds that *"surrender is the simple but profound wisdom of yielding to rather than opposing the flow of life"* and that *"the only place where you can experience the flow of life is the Now"*. Therefore, *"to surrender is to accept the present moment unconditionally and without reservation; it is to relinquish inner resistance to what is."*

In sum, to surrender is to accept the present moment as it is, without complaints, without expectations, without comparing it with an ideal future or an ideal past which are the root of suffering.

Truth is, when times *"go wrong"* we tend to idealize and cling on to the idea of a *"better future"* or a *"better past"*, creating a *"gap between the demands or rigid expectations of your mind and what is...."*

"That is the pain gap" Eckhart Tolle warns:

"Acceptance of what is immediately frees you from mind identification and thus reconnects you with Being. Resistance is the mind."

LESSON VII

BENEFITS OF MEDITATION PRACTICE

"In recent years, the wisdom of these ancient teachings has been confirmed by scientific studies, which demonstrate that we can train our minds, change our brains, increase our well-being, and radically lessen such afflictive states of mind as anxiety and depression... Other studies have shown that meditation may lower blood pressure, slow the progression of HIV, reduce pain help break addictions, and even ward off the effects of aging..."

The Washington Post (10/04/2012)

ACCORDING TO RESEARCH, daily meditation practice provides increasing levels of wellbeing and inner peace, allowing us to view life from a new perspective and solve our daily problems in creative new ways.

This transformation, according to Maharishi Mahesh Yogi, is generated by the repeated practice of experiencing the Self or *"Ultimate Reality"*, which he also called the *"transcendental field of eternal Being"* or *"pure state of Being"*, as he stated in *"The Science of Being and the Art of Living"* (1963):

> *"The transcendental state of Being lies beyond all seeing, hearing, touching, smelling and tasting: beyond all thinking and beyond all feeling. This state of unmanifested, absolute pure consciousness of the Being is the ultimate of life... "Through constantly going into the realm of the transcendental and back out into the field of relativity, the familiarity with the essential nature of the Being deepens, and the mind becomes gradually more aware of its own essential nature.*
>
> *"With more and more practice, the ability of the mind to maintain its essential nature while experiencing objects through the*

senses increases. When this happens, the mind and its essential nature, the state of transcendental Being, become one, and the mind is then capable of retaining its essential nature –Being- while engaged in thought, speech or action..."

BENEFITS OF DAILY PRACTICE

A recent Mayo Clinic report stated the following:

"Meditation can wipe away the day's stress, bringing with it inner peace... If stress has you anxious, tense and worried, consider trying meditation. Spending even a few minutes in meditation can restore your calm and inner peace... Meditation can give you a sense of calm, peace and balance that benefits both your emotional well-being and your overall health. And these benefits don't end when your meditation session ends. Meditation can help carry you more calmly through your day and may improve certain medical conditions..."

The Mayo Clinic report mentions the following *"emotional benefits of meditation"*:

*Gaining a new perspective on stressful situations

*Building skills to manage your stress

Increasing self-awareness

Focusing on the present

Reducing negative emotions

The Mayo Clinic report also states that meditation may improve certain medical conditions "especially those that may be worsened by stress", such as:

Anxiety disorders

Asthma

Cancer

Depression

Heart disease

High blood pressure

Pain

Sleep problems

Regarding the effects of meditation on the process of "*aging*", according to an independent study published in 2012, scientists at the University of California at Los Angeles and Nobel Prize winner Elizabeth Blackburn found that 12 minutes of daily yoga meditation for eight weeks increased an improvement of up to 43 percent in "*stress-induced aging*". Blackburn of the University of

California, San Francisco, shared the Nobel medicine prize in 2009 with Carol Greider and Jack Szostak for research on the *"immortality enzyme"* (*telomerase*) known to slow the *"cellular aging"* process.

MEDITATION IS A PERSONAL EXPERIENCE

Meditation is always a personal, inner experience just like the mindful state of *"awakening"* it pursues. It is a practice, not a theory, and thus cannot be thoroughly understood nor explained through intellectual reasoning.

Meditation depends on inner practice, not on specific religious beliefs, dogmas, rituals nor attending temples, for the true Path dwells within you.

This is why Dalai Lama described the essence of Buddhist practice with these words:

> *"This is my simple religion. There is no need for temples; no need for complicated philosophy. Our own brain, our own heart is our temple..."*

EXERCISE SEVEN

DAILY MEDITATION PRACTICE

"Meditation is self-knowledge and without self-knowledge there is no meditation. If you are not aware of all your responses all the time, if you are not fully conscious, fully cognizant of your daily activities, merely to lock yourself in a room and sit down in front of a picture of your guru, of your Master, to meditate, is an escape, because without self-knowledge there is no right thinking and, without right thinking, what you do has no meaning, however noble your intentions are."

Krishnamurti

THIS LAST EXERCISE consists in setting up your schedule for daily meditation practice. These are some of the most frequent questions made by beginners at this stage:

How long should I meditate?

You can start out with several brief sessions of one or two minutes each and gradually increase them.

Maharishi Mahesh Yogi recommends two sessions: 20 minutes in the morning, after waking up, and 20 minutes in the afternoon or night, before going to sleep.

Do I need to meditate that long to start out?

Not at all! You can set up your own pace and routine. During the first days, for example, you can start out with two-minute sessions at least five or six times a day. As little as ten to fifteen minutes of total meditation practice per day should suffice to start to calm your mind and let you begin to experience the "silent gap" between thoughts.

Do I need to meditate in a special place?

Although you can prepare a special place to meditate at home, you can meditate practically everywhere: at school, in your office, while walking, eating, taking an elevator, waiting in line, driving, riding a cab, bus or train, etc. Of course, you can also meditate in a park, beach, mountain, forest, desert, and even in a crowded street, etc. As you will see, practically anywhere will do!

What about noise and distractions?

You don't need to avoid noise and distractions. You see, if you close your eyes and mentally repeat the mantra you can use all the sounds that surround you as a secondary focus of attention, including what you consider "*noise and distractions*"... Simply listen to your mantra and also listen to the sounds that surround you without thinking about them... And each time a thought arises, release the thought and once again concentrate on the mantra and the sounds that surround you...

Become the "*silent Witness*", pay attention to the mantra and the sounds in silence and try to experience the "*silent gaps*" between thoughts... By doing this, as practice evidences, you can turn any distraction into a secondary focus of attention that can actually help you attain mental stillness and inner peace.

Remember:

You don't need to seclude yourself or become a hermit if you wish to meditate. As Jiddu Krishnamurti rightly said:

> "*Many who seek quietness of mind withdraw from active life to a village, to a monastery, to the mountains, or they withdraw into ideas, enclose themselves in a belief or*

avoid people who give them trouble. Such isolation is not stillness of mind.

"The enclosure of the mind in an idea or the avoidance of people who make life complicated does not bring about stillness of mind. Stillness of mind comes only when here is no process of isolation through accumulation but complete understanding of the whole process of relationship..."

For best results, meditate as much as you can these first few days and gradually increase the length of each session.

Although you can actually begin to experience inner peace today simply by reading this book and doing its exercises, the key action for your future progress is ***PRACTICE, PRACTICE AND MORE PRACTICE!***

Om!

APPENDIX

MANTRA AND THE SILENT STATE OF THE MIND

Maharishi Mahesh Yogi:

The teaching has been set up in a very standard form. What we do is actual practice involves thinking of a word. A word devoid of meaning, with no meaning, we don´t want to know the meaning… Someone who doesn't know the meaning of the word pencil in English will just hear the sound "pencil"… the meaning is static.

The sound changes in its pitch—it can be loud sound, or low sound. The meaning is the same at every pitch, high or low.

If the mind is on the meaning, there is no chance of refining the meaning. If the mind is not on the meaning, there is a chance of refining the sound, there is a chance of experiencing the sound in its finer values till the finest could be transcended and the awareness could reach that inner wakefulness devoid of any perception.

This will be Transcendental Consciousness....

The thought functions as an impulse, as a motivation for impulse, then the mind is pulsating if we don't try to manipulate the thought or hold it on or anything then the thought will start to refine... refine... refine... and it will sink out and its activity will start to die out... die out... die out...

So this is what we say: Naturally, a greater activity of the mind reaches its least value in a very, very natural way.

Any activity has the tendency to settle down and be quiet.

So this natural tendency of the mind to be quiet is all we use in Transcendental Meditation, and nothing else.

So in a very innocent manner, we think of the thought and every time we think it becomes finer, finer and finer and we experience its finer thoughts and then it dies out.

The mind is left wide awake by itself without any sound to experience. That inner wakefulness is that unbounded awareness, no boundaries. This unbounded awareness where the perception is no longer within boundaries—it is unbounded.

This is a silent state of the mind, and it is so fulfilling that the physiology having tasted this kind of quietness of activity it cherishes that. And because it is cherishing to the whole physiology, to the whole experience, the physiology tends to maintain that state naturally even when there are activities.

So by nature that state is experienced, and by nature, through practice, it becomes stabilized in the field of activity....

The whole thing is very simple.

It is an absolutely natural process...

(Excerpt from the YouTube video: "Mantra and Transcendental Meditation Explained by Maharishi")

ABOUT THE AUTHOR

"MY SPIRITUAL JOURNEY"

(A. J. PARRA is an experienced journalist and indie author with a lifelong interest in meditation techniques and the Comparative Study of Religion)

After studying all my childhood and youth in Catholic schools, I became interested in Hinduism when I was only 17 years old (I am presently 59). That's when, without giving up my Christian roots and beliefs, I received my first Hindu initiation at the *Mission of the Divine Light*, founded by Guru Maharaj Ji (presently known as

Prem Rawat or Maharaji). His basic teachings, based on a mixture Hinduism, Buddhism and Christianity, included the notion of the *veil of Maya* as well as several meditation techniques to free the thinking minds from the world of Illusion.

I was 29 when I received my second Hindu initiation (and my first mantra-meditation technique, this time from a direct disciple of Maharishi Mahesh Yogi (1918-2008). Also known as *the Guru of the Beatles*, creator of Transcendental Meditation or TM, his technique was practiced, among others, by the Beatles, Mia Farrow, Shirley MacLaine, the Beach Boys, and Donovan and, to name a few.

I was 37when I received my third initiation and meditation technique. This time from a direct disciple of guru Sant Thakar Singh (1929–2005) of the Sant Mat tradition, also known as *"The Path of Saints"*. The Indian poet and saint Kabir (1440–1518) is said to have belonged to the first generation of Sant Mat, which´s roots derived from Hinduism and were influenced by Sikhism.

About a decade ago, attracted by the similarities between Christianity and the world's main religions, I started studying *"A Course in Miracles"* as well as the teachings of Eckhart Tolle. As a holistic Christian, I have been patiently researching and writing since then, combining my personal knowledge and experience to finally give birth to *"The Secret of Now Series"*.

THE SECRET OF NOW SERIES

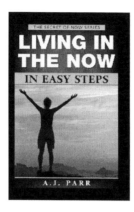

VOLUME 1

Living in "The Now" in Easy Steps

https://www.amazon.com/dp/B00J57TQZO

VOLUME 2

Buddhist Meditation For Beginners

https://www.amazon.com/dp/B00JE54A8K

VOLUME 3

Spiritual Hindu Tales to Calm Your Mind

https://www.amazon.com/dp/B00JJZLCBI

VOLUME 4

Christian Meditation in Easy Steps

https://www.amazon.com/dp/B00KLHUG7Y

VOLUME 5

Meditation in 7 Easy Steps

https://www.amazon.com/dp/B01L9DRF9U

VOLUME 6

Stop Negative Thinking in 7 Easy Steps

https://www.amazon.com/dp/B00MVLI6JI

PUBLISHED BY:

48801709R00080

Printed in Poland
by Amazon Fulfillment
Poland Sp. z o.o., Wrocław